Money Magnetism

MONEY MAGNETISM

How to Attract What You Need When You Need It

J. DONALD WALTERS

Crystal Clarity Publishers
Nevada City, California

Crystal Clarity Publishers, Nevada City, CA 95959
 Published 2000
First edition 1992. Second edition 1992. Third edition 2000

Printed in the USA
3 5 7 9 10 8 6 4 2

ISBN13: 978-1-56589-141-8

Cover photo by J. Donald Walters
Design by C. A. Starner Schuppe

Library of Congress CIP data:
Walters, J. Donald.
Money Magnetism: how to attract what you need when you need it /
J. Donald Walters.
p. cm.
ISBN-10: 1-56589-141-4
1. New Thought. I. Title.

BF639 .W18 2000
332.024—dc21

00-024073

www.crystalclarity.com
clarity@crystalclarity.com
800-424-1055

Contents

Part I
The Principles

Part II
The Method

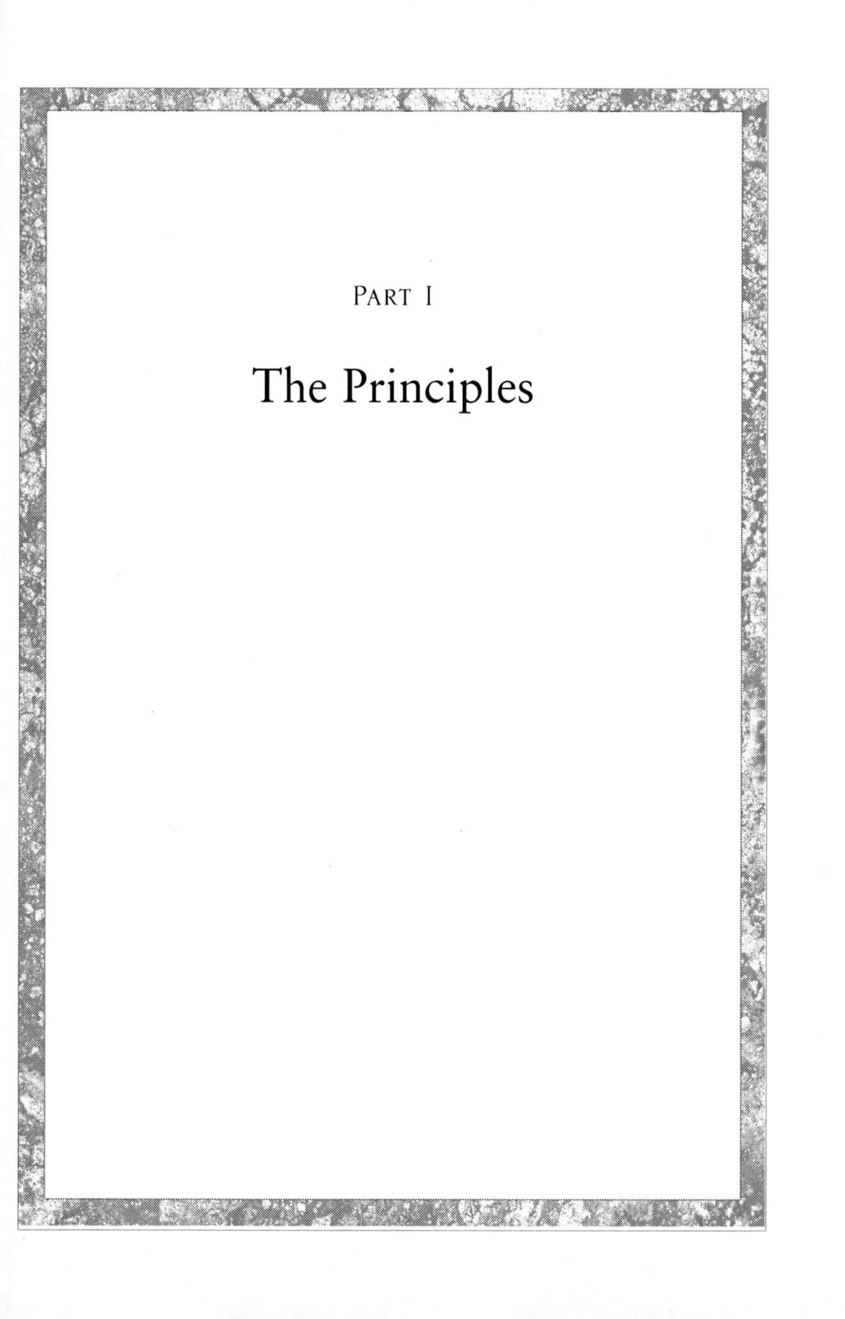

PART I

The Principles

Chapter One

What Is True Wealth?

Money, we've all heard, is the root of all evil. This piece of folk wisdom is due, no doubt, to the fact that so many people mistakenly imagine that money is the source of all good! For when we expect too much of anything, we eventually find, as with idol worship, that the object of our dependence is not competent to answer our prayers, nor capable of fulfilling our expectations of it.

Perhaps, then, that ancient saying should be amended to read, "*The love of* money is the root of all evil," as St. Paul said.

After all, money is not evil in itself, any more than dynamite is evil. Dynamite can be used constructively to build roads, or destructively to demolish buildings. Money, similarly, can be used to do wonderful things. It is human greed that so often directs money toward evil ends.

Money represents, quite simply, a flow of energy. Harm results when money is loved and hoarded for its own sake. For in hoarding it, we block the energy-flow.

A child once accompanied his

parents on an outing to the mountains. With them, he drank cool water from a mountain stream. Loving its fresh taste, he filled a bottle from the stream and took it home with him. There, he would sip only a little water each day, wanting to make it last as long as possible.

What was his disappointment a few weeks later, then, to find that the water left in the bottle had become stagnant.

Money, similarly, grows stagnant when we "bottle it up"—that is to say, hoard it. To attract a steady money-flow in our lives, we must learn to view money not as a thing merely, but as an expression of energy—ultimately, as an expression of *our* energy.

The three concepts that are suggested by the title of this book are interrelated, then—in fact, interdependent.

Developing money magnetism depends to a great extent on understanding how to use money properly.

Using money properly depends on realizing that, in *acquiring* money, we don't merely manipulate material forces in our favor. Still less is the acquisition of money a matter of luck. Rather, we attract money to us. The other side of that coin is that the failure to acquire money is essentially an act of repulsion on our part—

unconscious, to be sure. We may push it from us even while we imagine that we are doing our best to acquire it.

Both of these concepts—learning how to attract money, and how to put it to the proper use—depend, finally, on understanding what truly constitutes our *needs,* that is, our own, and others', highest good. For it is a law of life that when we waste any resource, we encounter a time finally when we can no longer replenish it. Think of the vast numbers of forests that have been cut without thought for replanting; of farmland that has been exhausted because its soil was never replenished.

Think of the many stories of movie

stars who, instead of using their money discriminately, squandered it until, at last, they were left penniless.

What is wealth? Most people equate it with investments, with savings, with income, with real property. Yet we've all known people who got by quite happily on very little money. I've known others, by contrast, who seemed barely able to scrape by, even though they may have earned several times as much as the first group.

The strange thing is that those who get by on very little often manage to obtain *more* of this world's goods, to go on more vacations, and to do a great deal in other ways that others with more money never seemed able to do.

Who among these, then, was the more truly wealthy? It isn't merely a matter of how much you have, but rather of how well you know how to use what you have. You know the song from Gershwin's *Porgy and Bess,* "I got plenty o' nuthin, an' nuthin's plenty fo' me"? In the last analysis, one is as wealthy or as poor as he thinks himself to be. Wealth cannot be equated with some fixed quantity. If one is wealthy in his mind, or in his spirit, he may require very few material possessions to be perfectly satisfied with life. If, on the other hand, one considers himself wealthy *only* for his material riches, he may be convinced he is poor even if he has fifty million dollars, perhaps only because some former classmate of his has ninety million.

I remember a time, in 1963, when an absence of income, combined with a determination to devote myself to writing a book (I eventually published it under the title, *Crises in Modern Thought*), led to my having to live for three months on only ten dollars a month. Today, instead of recalling that period of my life as a time of great privation and hardship, I recall it happily as a time of satisfying challenge and adventure.

During those three months, I

learned all sorts of tricks for living inexpensively. I sprouted alfalfa seeds. I made Indian chappatis instead of buying bread. I trained my palate to enjoy powdered milk, which is much cheaper than regular milk, and to be content with a single taste of dessert rather than filling myself on a bowlful of it. I took advantage of special sales at the local grocery stores. And I concentrated on preparing cheap, but high-energy, foods like split pea soup, which lasted me several days. No doubt one could say that I was poor then. Yet I didn't *feel* particularly poor. I won't go so far as to say that I felt rich, but the important thing is that, because I didn't dwell sadly on all the things I lacked, I really *wasn't* poor. I'll go farther: In every way that really mattered, I *was* rich.

There's the charming story of an American Indian who happily farmed a meager quarter-acre plot. A wealthy neighbor of his befriended him. One day this friend offered him five acres, to give him more land to farm. "Thank you for the gesture," the Indian replied. "But if I had more land to work, when would I find the time for singing?"

On the opposite side of this coin, I've known people with a great deal of money who could never convince themselves that they were even well off. And I recall a certain friend of mine in India, a scientist and a professor at a respected university. He owned his own home. His family and he ate well, dressed well, and lived reasonably well. Yet he considered himself wretched. His complaint was that he couldn't afford some of the expensive gadgetry he'd seen and enjoyed in the West—things like state-of-the-art television. I recall him weeping to me one evening, "I'm poor! I'm poor!"

Wealth is the *consciousness* of abundance. And poverty is the *consciousness* of lack. *Wealth and poverty are both states of mind.* You are as rich, or as poor, as *you* believe yourself to be.

I don't want my readers to think that I've lured them into reading a treatise on how to attract money only to substitute for it (having once got *their* money safely in my pocket!) a philosophy of self-deprivation. Money *is* important in this world. A person who writes books needs money to support himself while he writes. A photographer needs expensive lenses to take the best pictures. There is no field of activity in which money does not figure in some way. Nor do I suppose that I myself could have lived for very long on only ten dollars a month.

Essential to my theme, however, is the importance of the right mental attitude, not only for defining the parameters of happiness intelligently, *but also for attracting wealth in the first place.*

The purpose of this book is to help you to attract money in such a way as not to make it a burden on your peace of mind, but a doorway, rather, to genuine opportunity. It is to help you to learn how to use money wisely, in such a way as to acquire the greatest possible benefits for yourself and for others.

CHAPTER TWO

Seek Security within Yourself First

The teachings of Jesus Christ were intended primarily for the salvation of men's souls. Nevertheless, because truth remains true no matter on what level of reality we seek it, many of Jesus' sayings can be applied effectively even on ordinary levels of human life.

Take this saying, for example: "To him who has shall be given, and he shall have abundance; but from him who does not have, even that which he has shall be taken away." (Matthew 13:12) At first glance, this may seem a very unfair teaching, no matter on what level of truth we apply it. If, however, we think of abundance as something one *attracts* to himself, rather than waiting for it to be doled out to him by a whimsical Destiny—an uncertain blessing over which he has no control—then we can see that Jesus is addressing the issue in another spirit altogether.

Quite simply, what he was emphasizing was the importance of *our own* responsibility in the quest for abundance. Abundance, in other words, is something we must *draw* to us. Abundance of all kinds. For success, too, is a kind of abundance. So also is emotional fulfillment. So also are friends. We *draw* these to us. We can also repel them.

A *consciousness* of abundance attracts abundance. It's really that simple, though it may help to explain this principle a little further. A *consciousness* of poverty, on the other hand, attracts poverty.

You've probably heard people speak of "poverty consciousness." There is negative power in negative attitudes. Our expectations of life, whether positive or negative, determine to a great extent the wealth or poverty, the success or failure, the fulfillment or disappointment, that we receive from life.

An important point to consider is that we can increase or decrease the influence of these expectations by the intensity with which we focus our thoughts and feelings on them.

A cornerstone of the teachings of the great spiritual teacher, Paramhansa Yogananda, is the aphorism, *The greater the will, the greater the flow of energy.* Will power it is that directs energy to the body, and outward from the body toward any object of fulfillment. And the effectiveness of our expectations of life depends on the energy we focus upon them.

A person of weak will power will inevitably be also a person whose energy-flow is weak. By contrast, a person of great will power always finds reserves of inner energy from which he draws the ability to attain his objectives.

Willingness generates energy. Unwillingness, on the other hand, depletes one's supply of energy, no matter how much he tries to replenish it with sufficient rest and a good diet.

Energy is, indeed, the link between mind and body—between Divine Consciousness and the material universe. Science has demonstrated that matter *is* energy, essentially. Many leading modern physicists go further and state their belief that energy is a manifestation of consciousness. In this they concur with the ancient teachings, which state that the Divine Will manifested the material universe through the medium of cosmic energy.

When we direct our hand to raise, say, a stone, we do so not merely by visualizing it as raising the stone. We also send *energy* to it by the command of our will, and we direct the energy to raise the stone.

Yogananda created a set of psychophysical exercises to develop a person's awareness of, and control over, this flow of energy in the body. I myself have practiced this system of exercises daily for many years, and have found it to be enormously beneficial not only physically, but also in its application to the principles being discussed here.

Even without this system of exercises, one can acquire great power to influence events that more passive people think of as beyond our control. He can exert this power by simply understanding the influence of right attitude over the flow of energy. For energy doesn't merely act upon matter through the muscles of our bodies. It exerts a *magnetic* force *beyond our bodies* to *attract* to us whatever we want (or, just as effectively by strong negative expectations, what we don't want) in our lives.

Energy may be compared to electricity. Indeed, electricity *is* a form of energy. (Yogananda called it, quaintly, "the animal current in the energy world.") Electricity is a lower manifestation of the same energy as that which moves the body. It is a particular manifestation of the cosmic energy which created the material universe.

When electricity flows through a wire, it generates a magnetic field. The stronger the flow, the more powerful this field.

Similarly, whenever we will something to happen, or to be drawn to us, a ray of energy goes out, projected by the power of our thought, or will. The energy, in its turn, generates a magnetic force-field. It is this magnetic force that attracts to us the object of our expectations.

Thus, to attract money, we must be confident that we have a right to our fair share of the abundance of the universe. And, indeed, we have that right, all of us.

Don't be passive in the demands you make on the universe. Don't wait for good fortune to smile on you. Be secure in yourself, and know that you, yourself, are an integral part of the cosmic reality.

When you have that consciousness

of living already in abundance, then, as Jesus said, you will attract more abundance.

CHAPTER THREE

Don't Limit Your Demands

There is a story of a man who died and was being shown around heaven by St. Peter. They came to what St. Peter called the "heavenly junk yard."

"Here you'll find all the gifts from heaven," he explained, "that people on earth rejected."

"Why, that's impossible!" explained the newcomer. "Some of

these things are beautiful. Look at that Cadillac over there. Who could possibly have rejected that?"

"Well, it's interesting that you should ask about that particular car," replied St. Peter. "As it happens, the person who rejected that Cadillac is *you.*"

"Impossible!" protested the other. "I'd never have refused such a wonderful gift."

"All the same, it was you. You see, the Cadillac was ready and waiting to be delivered to you. But every time you prayed for a car, you kept visualizing a little Volkswagen."

Most of the books I know that teach people how to actualize their ideas stress the importance of visualizing clearly the exact description, complete to size and shape, of the thing they want. Do they want a car? Then see the exact model car they want, its color, its shape; visualize it sitting in their garage, perhaps even with the keys in the ignition.

The point of the above story, then, is that it is not possible to anticipate in advance all the opportunities life holds in store for us. By demanding one specific opening, we may inadvertently fail to notice another.

We have already described money as an energy-flow. A flow of any kind is incompatible with rigidity, whether of ideas or of behavior. Dogmatic thinking is brittle thinking. Preconceived notions of how things *ought* to work may serve us well as long as everything develops along predictable lines. But they betray us whenever we find ourselves confronted with new challenges. A skier will fall if, on finding himself suddenly needing to make a right turn, he finds himself already committed to turning left.

In an energy-flow, one doesn't think of fixed stopping points. One thinks of continuous movement—beyond the known and visible to the unknown and invisible. One thinks not of fixed goals, but of continuous progress, continuous expansion toward ends that are lost in infinity.

In my life, I have often had to put this principle to use. Rarely have I found it helpful to have too specifically in mind some physical *thing* that I wanted. What I visualized, rather, was the *direction* I needed to move in. Clarity was indeed necessary, but it was necessary for me not to bind clarity in bonds that were too material.

Had I wanted a car, then, what I would have done—what I *have* done—is visualize clearly the service a car would give me, rather than the specific vehicle itself.

For the principles we're discussing are non-material principles. They are predicated on the fact that matter itself is only energy, and on the further concept that energy itself is only a manifestation of consciousness.

There have been a few times when I needed specific sums of money. At such times, naturally, I visualized the particular sum needed. However, even then I didn't visualize the money sitting there in a pile: green hundred-dollar bills on my desk, just waiting to be counted. Rather, I visualized the particular purpose this money was meant to serve. I concentrated on the energy-flow of which the money was a part, rather than on the money as a separate reality in itself.

The community where I live once held a rally during which everyone was asked to pledge varying amounts to beautify the "downtown" area, as we called it. They were asked to donate to specific projects: $100 for a tree, $25 for flowers for a flower-bed, and so on. One of the donations requested was $2,000 to improve the road. Looking at that sum, I thought, "No one will pledge such a large sum." As it happened, I myself didn't have any money for such a project. But I thought, "The roads *do* need improvement. So let me pledge that amount." I had no idea where the money would come from.

Beyond putting my pledge in an envelope, I said nothing about it to anyone. The payment on it was due in two weeks. A week later—I still had no idea where the money would come from—I awoke one morning to find an envelope under my door. It contained a letter from a friend I hadn't seen in a long time, who wrote, "I was just visiting here. My mother died a few months ago, and I've been wanting to give you something in her name, and in gratitude for help that you've given me through the years." Along with his letter was a check for $2,000.

If this sort of thing happened only once, you'd chalk it up to coincidence. But I've seen it happen again and again, to the point where coincidence simply has to be ruled out. Some definite principle is at work.

This very book, indeed, is an attempt to present principles that I've tested for many years, and proved.

Be flexible in your expectations. Otherwise you may find, even in the realization of your expectations, that what you attract isn't really what you needed, or else turns out to be much less than what you could have had.

Be *directional* in your expectations. Don't think of fixed goals, but rather think in terms of directional development.

And then, as I said in the last chapter, put energy into your creative visualization. Energy itself flows more forcefully when you think of it

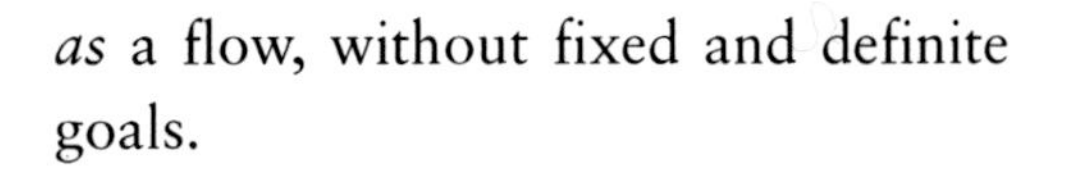
as a flow, without fixed and definite goals.

CHAPTER FOUR

You Are Part of a Greater Reality

If you removed the strings from a guitar and stretched them between two sticks, then tried to pluck them, you'd get only a very thin sound. Their tonal richness when plucked on a guitar is due to the guitar's sounding board, which augments their sound.

The same is true for the human ego. If we think of ourselves as solitary islands in a vast and disinterested ocean, we find ourselves threatened by life, not sustained by it. We may feel that we must claw and scratch our way up any hillock of difficulties that we face, and shout ourselves hoarse in the face of massive indifference to achieve even the least goals for ourselves.

Thus, people by the time they're forty are often a spent force already, psychologically exhausted, depleted in energy, ill much of the time, and cynical about their chances for future success: all because they've stretched their egos between two fixed points—say, their home and their job—rather than affixing them in greater awareness to the vastness of life and of the universe. Their interests are narrowly focused on "I, my, me, mine." They think in terms only of what they can get from life, not of what they can share with life and with others in the great adventure of existence.

If all this seems too vague for clear understanding, let's pin it to a specific example. Someone who goes through life thinking only of his own interests is far less likely to attract help from others than one who tries to involve others in his interests. Someone who tries to involve others only in his own interests is less likely to interest them than one who shows an interest also in what interests *them*. And one who approaches projects only from a standpoint of selfish interest, whether his own or other people's, is less likely to stir a sense of dedication either in himself or in them than one who appeals to high principles and ideals.

The broader our vision, the more powerful it will be.

I had a little demonstration of this truth years ago in Paris. The "broader" vision, in this case, was almost trivial, but for that reason it may be easier to grasp it.

It was my birthday, and I wanted to celebrate the occasion in some special way. A concert was announced in the papers that I decided fitted my definition of a celebration. I arrived at the church where the concert was to be held, however, only to find the official in charge closing the door on a crowd of about fifty people because, he announced, all the seats had been taken.

Dismayed to find my celebration in danger of becoming a fiasco, I cried out, "But it's my birthday!"

The official, faced with my appeal to this broader issue, one to which everyone can relate, called back, "*Alors, Monsieur,* come in. And happy birthday!" It's a small example, but it illustrates how often, when we take broader issues into account, we can open doors that are closed to us as long as we concentrate only on our own narrow intentions.

More is involved, however.

You may have read the book, or seen the movie, *The Fountainhead,* by Ayn Rand. On the surface, it's an attractive philosophy: one man standing firm in his convictions, loyal to his ideals, alone against the crowd. But as stated, the philosophy doesn't work.

Yes, we must be true to our ideals. Implicit here, however, is the concept of ideals as something greater than we are. Truth itself is infinitely greater than we are. If truth is the sounding board with which our whole being resonates, then what does it matter if all men rise up against us? What, indeed, is the entire human race but a swarm of ants before the immensity of Truth—timeless, infinite? Great men and women who lived by high principles gained far greater power from their attunement with them than they'd ever have gained by compromise with the mere opinions and interests of others.

What made *The Fountainhead* so ultimately fragile a statement was that its hero, the fearless architect, thought only in terms of his own *opinions* about architecture, of his own personal desires and fulfillment. A truth must be perceived: It cannot be created. Opinions are altogether different from perception. And desires that exclude the welfare of others are selfish, and therefore by definition small in scope.

Ayn Rand's philosophy never rose above the level of egoism: "My opinion and desires, firmly stated, against spineless compromise with the opinions and desires of others." The power to attract money, and success of every kind, increases in direct proportion to our ability to recognize, and attune ourselves to, a greater reality than our own.

CHAPTER FIVE

You Are Part of an *Intelligent* Reality

One of the great scientific discoveries of this century is the absence of dividing lines between animate and inanimate matter. For the first half or more of this century materialists had the serve in their court. They insisted that this discovery proved their claim that matter is the ultimate reality: that consciousness itself is merely the product of material factors, a sort of activation of energy patterns in a circuit of nerves.

Undermining their philosophy from the start, however, was the discovery, made early in this century, that matter is a manifestation of energy. Thus, the very material "realities" on which the materialists based their faith are insubstantial.

If matter and consciousness are in fact one, as indeed they appear to be, and if matter itself is without substance essentially, an opposite conclusion suggests itself: namely, not that consciousness is a material reality, but that consciousness is the abiding reality, whereas matter is merely a manifestation of consciousness.

If this is so, we find ourselves dealing with higher levels of involvement than most people imagine. That is to say, whatever we put out to attract money, or anything else, has something or someone else on the other end, helping us.

Many people who have no problem with John Donne's classic reminder, "No man is an island," may balk at the idea that surrounding them is an intelligent ocean. And many people who can accept that there is intelligence everywhere still find it difficult to imagine that this intelligence pays any special attention to *them*, personally.

Yet experience endorses the scriptural teaching that we *are* listened to.

The fact is, our intelligent awareness is an integral part of the vast, intelligent consciousness that underlies all things. When, in conscious attunement with that infinite consciousness, we draw on it, rather than acting as though all our thoughts and actions took place in a sort of spiritual vacuum, many things happen that we could never cause to happen by our own limited intelligence and will power. First, we receive inspiration from the infinite intelligence of which we are all a part. And second, we also involve that intelligence in whatever it is we try to do.

We don't have to figure out exactly how our goals will be achieved. Indeed, the less we bother with the particulars, provided we try at the same time to involve the Infinite Intelligence (you'll note I've capitalized it now, because by this time it must be clear that the Intelligence involved is what we've always called God), the more perfectly things seem to work out for us. Other factors come into play over which we could not possibly have any direct, personal influence.

The lives of saints are rich with examples of what most people, unaware of subtler levels of natural law, call miracles. In fact, there are no such things as miracles. This is simply the way the law works. The more one works in harmony with the Infinite Intelligence, the better everything works out for him. The more, on the other hand, one cuts himself off from that great Intelligence and struggles to make everything happen by his egoic power alone, the less power he has to make anything happen really well for him.

This truth is inspiring. However, it implies a responsibility to live in an expanded awareness. It is resisted, therefore, by the ego, which owes its very reality to its narrow identification with the body and personality. Thus, echoing countless jokes of our times, this chapter contains good news, and also bad news. The good news, of course, is that we have infinite power available to attract anything to us that we could possibly want. The bad news is that the more we want selfishly for ourselves, the less connection we'll have with that power.

For there are two directions in which our consciousness can move. The one is toward expansion. The other is toward contraction. There are no limits to our potential for expansion: We are already integral parts of infinity itself. Nor are there any limits to our potential for contraction. The contractive consciousness can cause us literally to collapse inward upon ourselves: through selfishness, pettiness, meanness, to a total lack of conscience, mental indifference, dullness, stupidity, unawareness, coma. Infinity has no more limits inwardly, toward the infinitesimal, than outwardly, toward the farthest reaches of cosmic reality. Human consciousness is capable of shrinking endlessly toward unconsciousness, once it sets its direction on a contractive course. The only thing it cannot achieve is *total* unconsciousness, for the simple reason that the only reality *is* consciousness.

We face an eternal choice, and it isn't an easy one. Often, past conditioning influences us to prefer escape into relative unawareness—by drink, for example, or by simply refusing to face reality—rather than accept the challenging call to infinity. We feel comfortable with the little ego, as a caged bird feels comfortable with its cage. We want to draw from whatever source we can—from infinity? sure, no problem!—to gratify our own little desires, but the thought of offering those desires into a higher reality makes us not merely uncomfortable: We rebel at it.

The fact is, to live truly by the high truths presented in this little volume, we must offer ourselves up to be used by them. We cannot simply use them to our own selfish ends, for the simple reason that selfishness runs counter to that reality.

Yet the "bad news," as I called it above, is really good news also. For although by contraction we cut ourselves off from that expansive reality, in contraction we cannot find in any case the fulfillment we promise ourselves in clinging to the ego, whereas in expansion of self-identity we find true fulfillment even on an egoic level. The higher law embraces the lower. The ancient Hermetic teachings put it this way: "As above, so below." Jesus also said, "Seek ye first the kingdom of God and His righteousness, and all these things shall be added unto you." (Matthew 6:33)

People imagine that living for God means giving up human fulfillment. In fact, all it means is giving up *attachment* to human fulfillment. Even if one wants only human fulfillment, he can attract it best by not being attached to it. To attract money, one important rule is not to be attached to money. For everything in life is like quicksilver: Grasp it, and it flies out of your hand. The way to hold it is simply to accept it, as you would cup your hand, but not to try to tighten your grip on it. Another way of looking at attachment is to think of it as inflexibility to adapt to change. Only the person who can adapt easily to change, who can adjust easily to new developments, who can remain open to new ways of looking at doing things, will be able to ride the waves instead of crashing with them when they crash.

There is an ancient saying in India: *Jato dharma, tato jaya:* Where there is right action, there is victory. To live in tune with high principles, don't imagine that you can twist them to your own ends. The highest realities are not merely intelligent, but infinitely wise. Adjust to them; don't imagine that they can be fooled by rationalizations, as people manage so often to fool themselves. Live by the truth, and it will serve you far better than you could ever serve yourself.

The more you include in all your striving a desire for the good of others along with your own welfare, the more you will thrive. Living for an expanded reality means to include what is best for others, not only for yourself. It isn't enough to embrace expansion on an abstract level. Your expanding awareness must include present, concrete realities: people, for example, whom you know and don't necessarily like; businesses which circumstances have inclined you to treat as rivals; strangers for whom you feel no particular human bond; animals, even; and issues where the desires of others may run counter to your own.

Cosmic Intelligence, God, is not

only conscious: It is conscious of *you*. It is conscious *as* you. You can pray to it and receive answers, guidance, and help from it. If you feel uneasy praying to your own higher Self, think of it as reaching up toward your own highest potential, which is conscious of your striving toward it, even if you are not conscious that it is ever there, waiting patiently for you to discover that level of reality in yourself.

Ask that greater Reality, then, "Guide me, that I make the right choices." Paramhansa Yogananda wrote this beautiful prayer in his book, *Whispers from Eternity:* "Father Divine, this is my prayer: I care not what I may permanently possess, but give to me the *power to acquire at will* whatever I may daily need."

CHAPTER SIX

How Much Wealth Is Available?

When we see someone with great wealth, we may think—many do—that he owns it at the cost of other people's prosperity. One of the assumptions in modern social thought is that there is just so much money to go round. If one person has more of it, others must necessarily have less.

This line of thinking is typical of the materialistic consciousness by which mankind was, until recently, ruled, but out of which the human race is now emerging. If we think of matter as the fundamental reality, we live perforce in a world of rigid limitations. Inevitably, then, we see supply of any kind as a fixed quantity, whether it be money, or energy (which we identify with the amount of oil left in the ground), or opportunity.

If, however, we think of consciousness as the reality that underlies everything, then we see quantity itself as circumscribed by nothing but the limitations of our own thinking.

In fact, as is well known, wealth is something we *create*. It is not merely there, waiting for us to find it and lay claim to it. Thus we see that it isn't only that we attract money to us: We attract *energy,* which then manifests itself in the form of money. And the supply of energy is cosmic in scope. Wealth isn't produced out of the ground, or out of a factory. It is produced out of the cosmic "ground" of being; out of the infinite "factory" of ideas.

In this volume I haven't even addressed one of the issues that one commonly encounters in treatises on how to grow rich: namely, to concentrate on making money the way an artist concentrates of creating paintings; to turn money-making, in other words, into a virtual art-form. Nor have I paid the usual attention to the *accumulation* of wealth.

The thing is, such an emphasis, though it is indeed a means of acquiring and keeping wealth, is ultimately self-defeating.

For one thing, as I pointed out earlier, wealth is much more than money. It is happiness, peace of mind, the richness of fulfilling relationships, a simple and uncluttered life, wisdom, love. To devote too much energy to the quest for money may make one "filthy rich," but it won't make one wealthy in the truest sense.

For another thing, the excessive accumulation of money deadens one's consciousness of it as energy, and heightens one's awareness of it as a fixed material reality, limited in quantity no matter how much one accumulates, and therefore ever in danger of being depleted, stolen, or lost in a market crash. The simple fact is that the more people have, usually, the more fearful they become of losing what they have. They accumulate money to gain a sense of security, and very often feel less secure in its very possession than they did when they had so little that attachment to what they had was not yet a temptation. The best course, where money is concerned, is to seek to attract as much of it as one needs, but not to try to become a multi-millionaire. The strain isn't worth it. Without balance in everything, including our search for material prosperity, we quickly reach a point of diminishing returns.

As long as we have the consciousness of hoarding—of taking for ourselves and never allowing the energy to flow through us to others—we block that energy flow; in time, it may cease altogether. A spring that is left unused will eventually cease flowing. The same is true of our spirituality: One who doesn't use his energy creatively finds its flow diminishing, and gradually dying. This is what Jesus meant when he said that the person who buried his talent in the ground, instead of using it, displeased his employer. The moral: If we hoard for ourselves instead of allowing the energy within us to flow outward, we displease the God deep within ourselves.

In conversation once with a well-to-do relative, I remarked how strange it seemed to me that people would spend all their money on themselves. I wasn't thinking of my relative's wealth at the time, and had no ulterior motive in saying what I did. Our discussion had simply touched on an expensive house that we'd seen described in the papers. But her reply astonished me. "Well," she exclaimed, "*that's* a novel thought!" The contrast between our two totally opposite attitudes, and the surprise occasioned both of us, highlighted for me the extent of the difference between the laws of the Spirit and those of the world.

A person who receives from God the blessing of great wealth, but spends it only on himself, will sooner or later find his wealth being removed from him, or its supply drying up. Whatever we are given in this world, whether money, popularity, or talent, should be taken as an opportunity for service. We were not put here on earth merely to live for ourselves. We were given the blessing of a human body that we might enter into a greater awareness of all life.

Materialistic people often think not only of matter, but of energy, too, as a limited quantity. The truth is, however, that the more you *use* your energy, the more you'll find that you *generate* energy. So many people think, "But I've got to save my strength." They are wrong.

Yes, of course we need rest, periodically. Yes, of course we mustn't overdo; we'd be foolish to drive ourselves to the point where our will power shuts off, for with unwillingness our energy supply shuts off, too. But remember: *Energy used joyfully and willingly doesn't exhaust energy;* it *generates more energy.*

If, then, you want to earn money,

approach it as a focal point for your energy-flow, and use it to help you generate a greater flow of energy. Remember, money is only a symbol of energy. Approach it *as* energy. And remember the principle, "The greater the will, the greater the flow of energy." There need be no limits to your flow of abundance. The only limits will be those you place on that flow yourself, by the self-erected fence of emotional attachment.

CHAPTER SEVEN

To Live Wisely, Give

The other day someone was telling me that certain friends of his had been talking to him about divorce. He said they'd remarked, "One shouldn't worry about the children. Just take care of yourself. If divorce is what *you* want, forget what it means to anyone else. *You* are the one you have to satisfy. The kids'll get by somehow." There is a lot of talk like that these days, isn't there? One finds it even in many teachings that are supposed to offer people some sort of enlightenment—"self-actualization" seminars, and the like. The most popular best-seller a few years ago was titled, *Looking Out for Number One.*

But theirs is a false teaching. And it is false primarily for one reason: that whatever shrinks one's awareness narrowly down to one's self, and focuses attention inward upon the little body and ego, instead of expanding it outward in sympathy toward others, must in the long run give one, not fulfillment, but pain.

Why is this so? Because the basic instinct of life is the desire to *expand* our identity, our awareness—our dominion, if you will, though he mistakes this instinct who thinks to satisfy it by increasing his possessions. We want to know more, which is why we read, why we study and travel, why we are curious about new things and listen to the radio to find out what people are doing in other parts of the world. The very basic impulse of life is to reach outward, and anything that denies this impulse denies, in the long run, the very reality of our nature. Thus, although one may experience for a time a certain pleasure in personal gain at the expense of others, in the end this kind of "pleasure" always leads to suffering.

Pain accompanies any shrinking of

identity, sympathy, or awareness. And anything that expands these inevitably gives us joy. Hence Jesus' saying, "It is more blessed to give than to receive"—more blessed, because more blissful. Giving wins happiness for the giver. If you really want fulfillment for yourself, if you really want to "look out for number one" in the best way, include in your own good the welfare of others.

The ability, then, to earn money, like all other talents, should be offered in service—upward to God, and outward to God in one's fellowman. Remember, this advice is for one's own fulfillment. Don't imagine that you deprive yourself when you identify yourself with a greater reality. You'll find that, on the contrary, service to any high ideal ensures you the greatest possible happiness.

Strange, that so many people equate service with humiliation and pain! That so many see fulfillment in terms of "getting theirs"—at the expense of everyone else! That so many offer as proof of their virtue the very pain they derive from it! A woman may work her fingers to the bone serving her husband and children, and get a sort of diseased comfort from her misery—as though it alone proved her goodness! Well, doing her duty as she sees it may in fact be right action, for her. And I grant you, should you take her side, that one should adhere to right action even in the teeth of suffering. Nevertheless, it remains true that the ultimate test of virtue is that it gives joy, not pain. And the test of sin is that, ultimately, it gives sorrow. We are blessed, the more we share of our abundance, the more we give, the more we serve. We are blessed!

CHAPTER EIGHT

The Value of Tithing

One very interesting principle, and an old idea in Judaism and Christianity, is that of tithing. This principle is that whenever you offer something to God, that offering becomes blessed. To the extent that you offer yourself to God, to that extent *you* become blessed.

There is a fascinating story from the life of Edgar Cayce, the renowned psychic. It is widely believed that he had the power to know people's past lives. At any rate, he once gave a past-life reading for a successful model. Her hands, particularly, were so beautiful that photographers often concentrated especially on them. Edgar Cayce, in a trance state, told her that in her last incarnation she had been a nun, and had spent much time on her hands and knees in the convent, scrubbing floors for God. Because she had used her hands devotedly in God's service, in her next life her hands were especially beautiful.

This story illustrates a truth that each of us can test in his own life. Have you a talent? Whatever it is, try offering it to God. Never mind if it doesn't seem to you like much of a gift. Do you remember the legend of the poor girl in church who put an apple in the collection plate—and how the apple turned to gold?

I recall a temple I once built. A year later, someone left a candle burning on the altar, and the temple burned to the ground. I won't go into the poor timing of this event, except to say that it happened barely a month after I'd succeeded, with much difficulty, in overcoming another serious financial hurdle. The timing, in other words, could hardly have seemed worse. Well, I sat in prayer after this conflagration, and told God, "This was Your temple, Lord, not mine. I gave it to You when I first built it. I've lost nothing, because I had nothing to lose."

Suddenly I felt overwhelmed from within with a joy so great, I could hardly bear it. "Lord," I then prayed, "if the destruction of a mere temple can bring me so much joy, You should have taken all my other possessions, too!"

I recall entering a shop later that day. I was singing. The shop-keeper, who had heard of our loss, exclaimed, "You're singing! When our shop burned down several years ago, I cried for one year." "Well," I answered, "I've lost a building, but I haven't lost my voice!"

The truth was, I *felt* like singing. God's joy within made everything else seem unimportant.

Indeed, if one gift can bring blessings, is he not wise who gives *everything* to God?

There is an inspiring poem by Rabindranath Tagore, the great Indian poet. It is so pertinent here that I'd like to quote it.

> I had gone a-begging from door to door in the village path, when thy golden chariot appeared in the distance like a gorgeous dream and I wondered who was this King of all kings!
>
> My hopes rose high and methought my evil days were at

an end, and I stood waiting for alms to be given unasked and for wealth scattered on all sides in the dust.

The chariot stopped where I stood. Thy glance fell on me and thou camest down with a smile. I felt that the luck of my life had come at last. Then of a sudden thou didst hold out thy right hand and say, "What has thou to give me?"

Ah, what a kingly jest was it to open thy palm to a beggar to beg! I was confused and stood undecided, and then from my wallet I slowly took out the least little grain of corn and gave it to thee.

But how great was my sur-

> prise when at the day's end I emptied my bag on the floor to find a least little grain of gold among the poor heap! I bitterly wept and wished that I had had the heart to give thee my all.

You see? It is in our own *interest* to give of our wealth to God. But how many can give all to Him? Most need to proceed slowly, testing the principle every inch of the way to make sure it still works! I'm not being sarcastic: We're all in the same boat. The truth is, our desires are locked up in our subconscious minds, where we can't easily get at them. An alcoholic may desire, consciously, to give up drinking, but his subconscious may keep pushing him in the old, accustomed direction. It takes time to dig out these long-buried roots. But still, the job is possible—desirable—in fact, *essential* if we are ever to know perfect fulfillment.

And I can attest personally that this principle works. I've discovered that, to an amazing degree, when we give everything to God He takes care of us.

To return to that story of the temple that burned down: At the time, it looked like a material loss, at least, even if it became a spiritual gain. In fact, however, it became a material gain also. Out of the loss of that one building came so many blessings, materially, that it would be difficult to count them.

Let me tell you a little story.

When I finished writing my home-study course, *The Art and Science of Raja Yoga,* a job that took me two solid years of work, I decided to go off and celebrate its completion with God. This is something I usually do whenever I've completed a project for Him, especially one that has required a great deal of time and effort. So I went to Carmel, a charming seaside town on the California coast.

Well, I didn't stop to consider that this was August, and the height of the tourist season. When I arrived,

I found almost no rooms available. Finally I did locate one, but it was renting at a much higher price than I could reasonably afford to pay. I hesitated. But then I thought, "Divine Mother, I've come here to celebrate with You. What shall I do? Shall I go find a motel nearby, in Monterey, with all the traffic and noise? Why settle for a half-baked celebration? Let me just go ahead and take this room. I'll leave it to You to see that I have enough money to get home." With that I took out my wallet to pay for the room. But the clerk at the desk, who didn't know me from any of the thousands of tourists who had come through Carmel that summer, shook his head.

"Don't pay me," he said.

"But I'd rather pay you now." I didn't add that I was concerned lest, by morning, I not have enough money left to pay the bill.

"I don't want you to pay me at all," he explained.

"But why not?"

"I'll just write you down in our books as a travel agent."

"Okay, then: *Why?*"

"I don't know," he said. "I just like you."

And then I understood: Because I was sharing this celebration with

God, God was also sharing it with me!

The following day I ate lunch in a restaurant. Afterward, the owner wouldn't let me pay for my meal!

Now, how many times have you gone to a motel or a restaurant and been told, "No, we don't want you to pay"? I can tell you how often it's happened to me: *once.* The only reason it happened then was that I had gone there with the conscious thought, "This is *our* celebration."

If you've never tried doing things *with* God before, try it. You'll be amazed at how, when you do things that way, He will be there doing them with you!

An effective way to learn this principle is by tithing—ten percent, traditionally—of your income, in God's name, to some good cause. Many people object, "I can't afford to give just now, but I'll be happy to give later on, when I *can* afford to." They don't realize that the very act of giving generates abundance. People who give selflessly to God find that He sustains them. Whatever energy they put out flows back to them, reinforced by the power that sustains the universe. As Jesus put it, "Everyone that hath forsaken houses, or brethren, or sisters, or father, or mother, or wife, or children, or lands, for my name's sake, shall receive an hundredfold, and shall inherit everlasting life." (Matthew 19:29) And as Sri Krishna puts it in the *Bhagavad Gita,* "Know this for certain: My devotee is *never* lost."

Friends of mine, a married couple, had been thinking recently of writing their church to say, "We really can't afford to tithe." Then they learned that other church members, who had considerably less money than they did, were tithing regularly. So they took heart and began tithing too.

Soon thereafter, one of them, who had been out of work, found a job. At about the same time, the other got a raise in pay!

If you tithe a portion of your income

to God, you will find that, far from depriving yourself, you will be blessed by the Source of all abundance, God. All real security comes from Him; until you understand and accept this truth, your path through life will forever remain uncertain. But the more you live for Him, the more you will find Him taking care of you—even in the smallest details of your life.

CHAPTER NINE

How Earning Money Can Promote Spiritual Growth

Once you learn to use money rightly, you will find gains on many levels. Your abundance, energy, joy—all will expand.

I had an interesting experience, many years ago. I undertook what was, for me, an important project. I was doing it for others. As things turned out (don't they *always* turn out that way?), it proved far more expensive than I first anticipated. I had, at first, to earn almost all the money for this project on my own. This meant going out and giving classes in many cities, and working harder than I'd ever worked before. It meant money worries I'd never had before. And it meant worrying that I was getting enmeshed in materialism—a serious concern for me, as I've always tried to live my life by higher, spiritual values.

It was only at the end of this long struggle that I discovered what my real gain had been. It was far more spiritual than material. True, I had earned lots of money. I had paid off the debts I'd incurred to finish the project. Beyond that, however, and inestimably more important to me personally, by doing what I had had to do and not shirking the challenge, and by doing it for others, not for myself, I found myself inwardly much stronger, more energetic, more confident of my ability to handle whatever challenge life chose to give me next. Above all, I felt closer to God.

During the process of earning the money to pay for that undertaking, it was a surprise to me, and a great reassurance, to come upon two statements by Paramhansa Yogananda on the spiritual aspects of money-making. The first of these was a promise he'd made to a student of his to the effect that, by helping his mission monetarily, the student would make more rapid spiritual advancement. The second statement was more general: "Making money honestly and industriously to serve God's work is the next greatest art after the art of realizing God." Whereas I used to look upon money-making as a rather sordid necessity of life, I've come to see the need for it as a great spiritual opportunity. Indeed, as I said earlier, my greatest gain from undertaking this project was the spiritual power, the faith, the will power and energy that this service gave me.

It is an interesting fact that many

businessmen, once they decide to devote their lives and service to God, make rapid spiritual advancement. Formerly, even if they used their energy selfishly, at least they *used* it! In the process, they learned to focus powers which they could now apply toward meditation and higher development. Such people come out far ahead of many who feel that they are more spiritual simply because they scorn involvement in earning money.

You see, it also takes energy to develop spiritually. Spiritual practices, such as meditation, are not passive practices. If one meditates properly, his efforts are dynamic. If you meditate with full awareness—

not restlessly, but alertly, putting all your concentration on what you're doing—you will advance far more quickly than if you sit absent-mindedly, trying to think good thoughts.

Whatever you do, therefore, put your full energy into it. If you have to earn money, don't work at it with half your mind, while, with the other half, regretting what you are doing. If you are in a position where you don't have to think about earning money—fine; you can direct your energy toward other things. But this is not necessarily better than for a person to be in a position where he has to think about earning money.

I visited a wealthy man once who

told me, as if to excuse his continued need to work and support his family, "That isn't my reality out there. My life begins when I get home, and can sit quietly in my meditation room."

I imagine he was trying to impress me. I found myself thinking, however, "What a pity, to waste all that time at work during which he could also be living in God!"

You see, it isn't really important what we do, so long as we see everything we do as an opportunity for service, for applying energy creatively, for working for the welfare of all, for expanding our sympathies and awareness, for attuning our consciousness to the Infinite Intelligence.

Remember, God is in money, too. God is in business. God is in the banks just as much as He is in the mountains and the clouds, and in temples and churches. And though it is, I grant you, more difficult to see Him in the marketplace, nonetheless, He is there. If you look deeply enough, you *must* find Him, wherever *you* are.

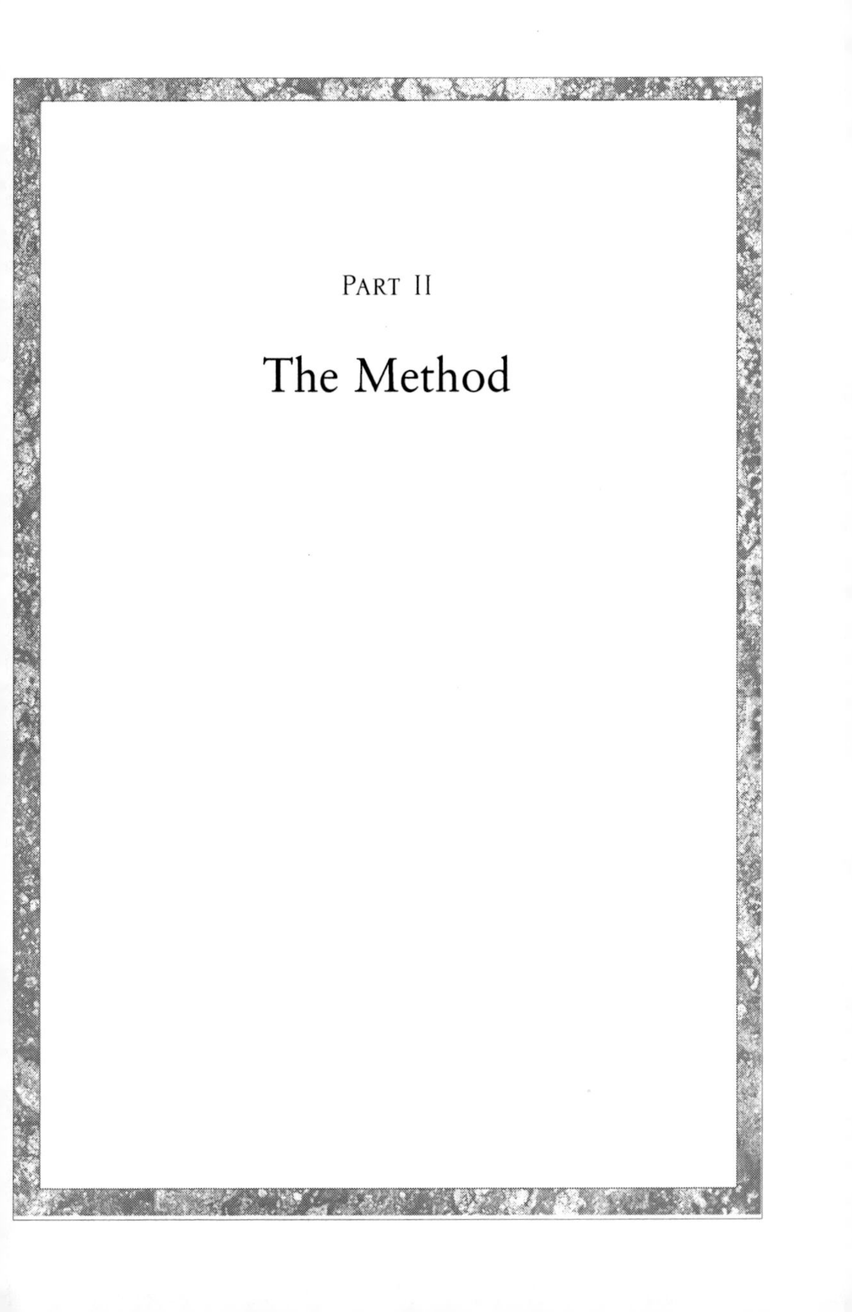

PART II

The Method

CHAPTER TEN

The Need for Concentration

So far we've discussed basic principles. Let us now consider a few practical suggestions for how those principles might be manifested.

The first point to consider is the need for *concentration.*

I mentioned earlier that success depends on the amount of energy we bring to bear on what we do. Will power, I mentioned also, directs energy. In the words of Paramhansa Yogananda, "The greater the will, the greater the flow of energy."

How, then, can one develop will power?

The first necessity is concentration. Concentration is like focusing diffused beams of light in a single laser ray. *Concentration is power.* When we can focus the mind one- pointedly, we are already far on the way to developing a powerful will.

It isn't enough, however, in this context, to imagine our mental forces as being limited to the functions of the brain. One's total consciousness includes also the heart's feeling.

The power of will, in fact, lies

less in what a person *thinks* than in what he *wants* to make happen. Thus, according to Paramhansa Yogananda's definition, "Will is *desire plus energy, directed toward fulfillment.*" Without feeling, what a person wills isn't able to rise above the level of abstraction. Without *focused* feeling, moreover, it will remain merely wishful thinking.

Feeling is that aspect of consciousness which empowers one's intentions. The feeling faculty must, at the same time, be kept *calm.* It must not be allowed to become restless or impatient.

When feeling fluctuates, it becomes emotion. Our emotions, too, may convey a sense of power. This sense, however, is fleeting and illusive. It is there one minute, then gone the next.

Emotions are like waves on the sea that move over the surface, while the water of which they are composed remains stationary. Emotions, in other words, have little lasting effect on the circumstances they touch. All they do is stir things up a little.

Again, like the waves, rising and falling, emotions, in their inconstancy, are self-canceling.

Another illustration springs to mind: a cartoon that appeared in the "New Yorker" many years ago, depicting a jeep that was traveling on a paved highway.

Jeeps in those days (during World War II, when jeeps were a new phenomenon) often were made a subject of humor. Usually, they were depicted two feet off the ground, bumping over rough terrain. In this particular cartoon, the jeep, though traveling along a smooth road, was *still* shown two feet off the ground.

That's how it is with uncontrolled feelings, with the emotions. Emotions whip up excitement in the heart, even when there isn't really anything to get excited about. The will doesn't, truly speaking, become will *power* until it is directed calmly, with control.

Without inner calmness and control, there can be no concentration.

By calmness I don't mean dullness of mind. The feeling faculty needn't be passive, to be calm. Rather, to be effective, one's feeling must be intense.

It is vitally important to summon up a strong feeling for what one wants to accomplish. As has been well said, nothing great was ever accomplished without enthusiasm. All that is needed, for feeling to generate strong will power, is to keep one's enthusiasm from spilling over in the form of excitement.

A tailor may want, he may even be enthusiastic, to create a beautiful dress. At the same time, he knows that, to thread the needle, he must perform that action with a calm and steady hand. If even one wisp of thread eludes the eye of the needle, he will simply have to remove the whole thread, draw it to a point again, and try anew.

In the case of will power, the thread may be compared to the feeling faculty. And the needle's eye is comparable to the seat of concentration in the body, the point between the two eyebrows. Feeling must be directed calmly through this "eye" before it is projected outward, toward one's objectives.

How, then, is one to control the feelings? A simple technique is to direct them upward through the

If you keep on trying, failure itself can be a doorway to victory.

The reader may ask: If all things change anyway, won't success come to us automatically anyway, without effort on our part?

The answer is: No. If you don't add your own conscious effort to the natural course of events, the force of circumstance that could have raised you to success will merely lift you a few inches. It may give you a minor sale, for example, whereas with right effort you might have closed the greatest deal of your life.

To catch the crest of a wave, a surfboarder knows that he must have balance, timing, and self-control.

channel of the spine to the brain, then through the brain to the point between the eyebrows.

To discipline the feeling faculty, remind yourself daily that all the conditions around you are inconstant. Be non-attached. Today's happiness can be lost tomorrow. Today's sorrow cannot but be replaced, eventually, by happiness. The wave-crests of joy and the troughs of depression alternate endlessly in the mind.

Look, then, to the longer rhythms. Look to the one constant that pervades all your life's experiences: your own consciousness, your own Self.

Become a cause, not an effect, of whatever happens in your life. Live at the center, not on the periphery, of your personal universe. Be who *you* are. Don't be an echo of other people's expectations and desires of you.

Be fully conscious of every act you perform.

Next, develop *staying* power. When you set your mind to accomplish something, no matter how trivial, don't give up on it until you've achieved your objective. Remember, just as our emotions—the way we react to, or the way we define, life's circumstances—are inconstant, so also are the conditions themselves forever changing. Change is the nature of this world. No failure is absolute.

Another perfectly normal question would be: If conditions are forever changing, won't success itself collapse around us eventually, no matter what we do?

The answer is, Yes, in a sense, but No in another, and much more important, sense. "Collapse" is in any case the wrong word, for if one wave of success sinks back from whence it came, other waves will certainly replace it. The important thing is that we not count on changing waves for our fulfillment.

What we really accomplish, in any case, with every victory is that we achieve victory *over ourselves*. Life's ups and downs cannot but alternate in ceaseless succession. The more we develop power over ourselves, however, the less any outer change will be able to affect us.

Ultimately, success is something one *becomes*, not something he *achieves*. Once a person becomes truly successful *as a human being*, he finds that everything that happens outwardly can be turned to good account. He need never be poor again. Everything becomes his gain.

CHAPTER ELEVEN

How to Develop Concentration

Concentration means being able to free the mind from all objects of distraction—including one's own thoughts and emotions—and to direct it toward a single object—whether reposing it in a single state of awareness, or directing it toward a single goal.

To many people, such mental control implies effort. And so it does, of course, in a sense. In another sense, however, they are mistaken. For as long as one *tries* to concentrate he will not be able to concentrate really effectively.

Deep concentration is possible only in a state of relaxation. Where tension exists, whether physically or mentally, there is a separate commitment of energy, like the stray strand of thread that refuses to enter the eye of the needle. If, for example, the brow is furrowed in worry, or if the jaw or the hands are clenched, these are signs that this much energy, at least, is not being directed toward one's true objective.

That is why the best way to develop

high-powered concentration is to practice meditation regularly.

Many people mistakenly believe that meditation amounts to a kind of escape from reality—an avoidance of one's worldly responsibilities. Actually, meditation is easily the most effective way of enabling one not only to face life's challenges, but to overcome them.

The deep power of concentration that comes through daily meditation enables a person to resolve an issue in minutes perhaps, where, otherwise, he might have fretted over it for weeks. Even more important, where the will is concerned, the concentration that comes due to regular meditation generates with perfect naturalness the strength of will that is necessary for success in any undertaking.

As I mentioned in the last chapter, the physical seat of the will is located at the point between the eyebrows. That is why, when a person wills something strongly, he often knits his eyebrows.

In meditation one is taught to concentrate at that point, since this is also the seat of concentration in the body. The more frequently and deeply one focuses the mind at that point, the more powerful his will becomes.

Another important point in developing concentration, and therefore will power, is inner clarity: crystal clarity of reason and feeling. Meditation is a great aid in the development of such clarity.

I've defined this state of crystal clarity in others of my books. Let me quote here what I've written in them:

> Crystal clarity means to see oneself, and all things, as aspects of a greater reality; to seek to enter into conscious attunement with that reality; and to see all things as channels for the expression of that reality.
>
> It means to see truth in simplicity; to seek to be guided always by the simple truth, not

> by opinion; and by what IS, not by one's own desires or prejudices.
>
> It means striving to see things in relation to their broadest potential.
>
> In one's association with other people, it means seeking always to include their realities in one's own.

Muddy thoughts and feelings produce chaos, both inwardly and outwardly. Inner confusion is the antithesis of concentration. Inner clarity, on the other hand, is almost the definition of concentration.

When the mind is clear, one naturally addresses issues one at a time. It is equally true to say that, by limiting oneself to doing or thinking about one thing at a time, one finds that the mind, in turn, gradually develops clarity.

Concentration, I said, involves, on the negative side, the practice of shutting out of the mind all distracting thoughts and impressions. It isn't easy *not* to think about a thing. Try telling yourself, for example, completely to avoid thinking about icebergs. How often, in the normal course of a day, does the thought of icebergs even occur to you? Never, probably, unless you live in arctic regions. Yet, if your mind is not practiced at concentration, the mere resolution *not* to think of icebergs may be sufficient to cause you to think of nothing else!

To develop concentration, then, it is more important to focus positively on one thing at a time than to avoid thinking of other things.

Try to become absorbed in one thought at a time. No one can do many things at once and do them effectively. Leave then, for the moment, every other issue except the one on which you've decided to focus your attention. Don't strain: Be relaxed. Be interested in what you are doing. Become absorbed in it.

When people go to the movies, they may find themselves becoming effortlessly absorbed in the story, simply because it has awakened their interest. Focus your mind like that on everything that you do.

Years ago, I and several friends were thinking of buying a building. At one point one of our group said, "I have the realtor's number." She held out to us the slip of paper on which she'd written the number. The conversation shifted temporarily to another topic. Fifteen minutes later, we finally decided to telephone the realtor.

"Let me get that number again," this friend said, taking out of her pocket once more the slip of paper.

"It's—." I told her the number.

She gazed at me in amazement. "Why, you hardly glanced at that number! How could you possibly have it memorized?"

"Really," I replied, "it's very simple. I didn't have to study it. All I did was look at it with concentration when you showed it to us."

My friend, afterward, tried following this suggestion in similar situations, and found that it worked infallibly.

Whatever we do, we should train our minds to do it with one-pointed attention. That doesn't mean striding grimly through life like a Man or Woman of Destiny. All it means, quite simply, is to be *interested* and *involved* in everything we do.

Do one thing at a time, and, as you do it, give it your full attention.

CHAPTER TWELVE

That Tricky Subconscious

It would be relatively easy to control the mind, were our conscious thought processes all we had to deal with. Unfortunately for this wished-for ease, the conscious mind is only the tip of a vast iceberg of consciousness. Buried in the subconscious, too deep even for conscious recognition, is a vast realm of unfulfilled desires and unresolved tendencies, which often militate against anything we try consciously to undertake.

A friend of mine was in Pakistan during the Indo-Pakistani war. Because Indian planes were strafing the highways, the bus in which he was traveling took a detour. At a certain point, the vehicle got stuck in a river bed.

The driver asked his passengers to get down and push the bus.

Fifteen minutes later, it hadn't budged an inch. Puzzled, the driver stepped back to assess the situation.

To his surprise, he found half the passengers pushing from the rear of the bus, as he'd wanted them to. The other half, however, were pushing just as strenuously from the front!

How often we display a similar tendency! Even though working earnestly, on one level of our consciousness, toward some desired end, on another level we manage to resist our own efforts.

While working hard, we may wish we didn't have to work at all. Perhaps, at the office, we indulge in "clock-watching." Or we may find ourselves day-dreaming. We may tell ourselves that our work is all useless anyway. Or we may waste energy by thinking of all the other things we'd rather be doing instead; or by thinking ahead to the hoped-for results of what we're doing, and not focusing on the task at hand.

We can accomplish a great deal in life, if we can discipline ourselves to do one thing at a time, to do it wholeheartedly, and not to worry distractedly about all the things we'd like to accomplish, or wish we had accomplished in the past.

An important aspect of crystal clarity, then, is not to work against ourselves, mentally. This, because of that large sub-continent in the mind, often proves to be easier said than done. In basic ways, every human being is like a house divided against itself. One part of our nature affirms life. Another part, disagreeing, rejects it.

Doubt, fear, and worry intervene to block even our best intentions.

There is in everyone, to however subtle a degree, a "no-saying" principle: a death wish; a wish to avoid issues rather than confront them; a wish to see one's problems simply disappear rather than have them continue to face him mockingly, demanding that he resolve them.

Some people seek escape in unconsciousness, through alcohol or drugs or excessive sleep. There is an actual pull on human consciousness to slip back into unawareness. Psychologists, especially in the first part of this century, made much of the conflict between what people think they *ought* to do and what they'd *like* to do. Because this conflict often produces inner complexes, born of suppression, psychologists—more often decades ago than today—counseled people to give in to their lower nature. It represented, they said, their *true* nature.

Nowadays, it is more generally understood that man's higher qualities are not merely his lower instincts disguised to look good. Love is not merely a sublimated sex-drive. It would be truer, indeed, to say that the sex-drive is an as-yet-unrealized, eternally spiritual hunger for perfect love.

It is an error to claim that the call to become a better human being is an imposition on us from without, by others—that it is a custom by which society tries to make us into something that, if we were completely honest with ourselves, we would recognize that we are not.

The call to raise our state of consciousness; to become more aware; to have more control over our lives; to be kind rather than unkind, or calm and forgiving rather than angry; proceeds from a recognition of our own inner potential. The duty to uplift ourselves is *self-imposed,* from within.

If society expects more of us than we seem ready to give, it is because other people, too, subconsciously recognize that all human beings have a higher potential, however much they have failed, so far, to explore them.

In giving free rein to our animal nature, we may silence, for a time, the imperatives of our lower, animal instincts. We cannot, however, revive ourselves from the sense of spiritual death that must forever haunt us, once we try to bury our higher, spiritual nature.

Nor—supreme irony!—can we, by giving in to our animal nature, silence thereby for very long the imperatives of that nature. It is true that, by giving in to our lower instincts, we may experience relief from their imperatives for a time. The very act of giving in, however, is tantamount to affirming that they have meaning for us.

People who vent their anger may, for a time, feel a release from anger. In no way, however, does the tendency toward anger release *them!* Each time they succumb to anger, what they do, in effect, is merely affirm anger as a viable way of dealing with trying circumstances.

The only way whereby succumbing to anger may actually be helpful to us is if we take advantage of the momentary relief, which venting may have given us, to affirm anger's oppositional states: calmness, forgiveness, love. If we direct the mind wisely, instead of letting it rule us, we can transform failure itself into victory. As Yogananda put it, "The season of failure is the best time for sowing the seeds of success."

To insist, however, that there is no victory to be won is to invite continual inner turmoil.

Our "complexes" cannot be resolved in mere surrender. To seek inner peace by embracing our lower nature—as even certain so-called "spiritual" teachers in modern times have suggested—is not very different from the operation known as prefrontal lobotomy.

Lobotomy used to be performed as a means of "resolving" a person's complexes, by cutting off entirely that part of the brain where the finer feelings reside. The patient was reduced thereby to the condition of a sort of household pet. He was free at last from extreme anxiety and other complexes, but was found to have lost his idealism, his sense of aspiration, and all those nobler qualities that separate man from the lower animals.

It is interesting that the qualities of concentration, calmness, self-control, and crystal clarity, which make it possible to develop strong will power, all reside in the frontal lobe of the brain—in that very portion of it which is severed in prefrontal lobotomy.

Concentration means exerting

oneself in a single direction, and not—as most people do all the time, whether consciously or unconsciously—working against oneself. To the extent that we can work on the conscious mind, the task is more or less clear cut. To the extent, however, that we must work on the subconscious to resolve those aspects of our nature which work against our active resolutions, we must reconcile ourselves to a more difficult, though still possible, task.

In fact, we must come to grips with the fact that we are, at all times, in the throes of an inner war.

That is why the great Indian scripture, the *Bhagavad Gita,* sets the

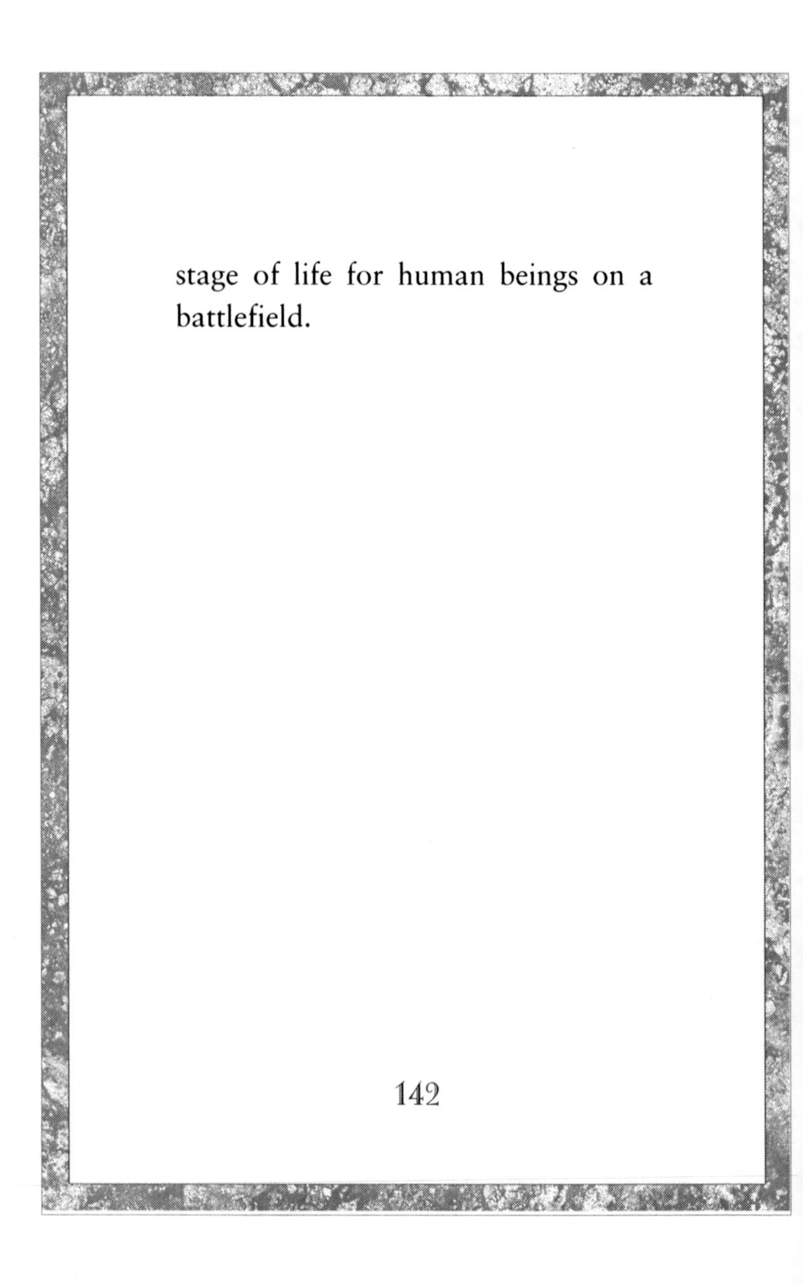

stage of life for human beings on a battlefield.

CHAPTER THIRTEEN

The Power of Affirmation

Many years ago, when I was twenty, I had the habit of smoking a pack or so of cigarettes a day. Shortly before I turned twenty-one, I decided to give up this unpleasant, yet at the same time too pleasant, habit. Unfortunately, as often as I gave it up I went back to it again. To refrain from smoking at the start of the day was easy enough. After lunch, however, while drinking coffee, I couldn't resist the thought that lunch wasn't really complete without a cigarette.

And so my case soon resembled Mark Twain's, who said, "Smoking is the easiest habit in the world to give up. I've done it a thousand times!"

Now then, if I'd felt, every time I broke my resolution, that I'd failed, my sense of failure might well have grown to the point where I might even have defined *myself* as a failure.

Instead, however, what I told myself after every failure was, "I haven't *yet* succeeded."

Thus, my affirmation became one of latent, though not yet actual, success.

After a year, as I went to bed one

evening I found that all those affirmations of delayed success had gathered together at last into a definite resolution. I told one of my roommates, who happened to enter the room at that moment, "I'm giving up smoking."

"Is that so?" he replied mockingly. "I've heard *that* one before!" With a light laugh he left the room.

But this time I was finally sure of myself. The next morning I awoke without the slightest desire for a cigarette. For two weeks thereafter, I kept my last remaining package of cigarettes in my breast pocket, passing them out to my friends. Never, from that day to this one, have I had the least desire for a smoke.

Failure, you see, comes only when we accept it as failure. We can just as easily, instead, make every failure a steppingstone to success. It's all a matter of how we look on failure. Instead of telling ourselves, "I've failed!" we should say, "I haven't *yet* succeeded."

When William the Conqueror landed at Hastings, the first thing he did was stumble and fall down. A gasp went through his army at this omen of disaster. William, however, a man of great will power, rose to his feet crying out, "I am so determined to conquer this land that, behold, I've seized it with both my hands!"

At that, a great shout of renewed confidence went up from every throat. William's army went on that day to win one of history's greatest battles.

A strong affirmation of will has the power to *impose* obedience on the subconscious. The important thing is to *address* the subconscious, and not merely to pretend that all is well in the ranks. The will must act like a general.

A military leader would be foolish to forge ahead in the mere hope that his soldiers will follow him. He must address them. He must stir them to faith in him and in his enterprise.

So must we do with our subconscious. It isn't enough to ignore its conflicting messages. We must inspire it to link hands with our conscious resolution.

Many people, I've noticed, will say something like, "I shouldn't have those qualities; therefore, *I don't have them.* I shouldn't be angry; therefore, it wasn't anger I just displayed: It was merely a justifiable impatience. I shouldn't be morally weak; therefore, I'm not to blame: It's others who were weak, and who inflicted their weaknesses on me."

Troops whose grievances go unrecognized may eventually become rebellious. So it is with the subconscious. We can't afford to ignore it. Nor, on the other hand, do we need to be led about by it, helplessly. We can command it.

In order to do so, we must face it squarely and honestly.

A general, again, doesn't need to know each and every soldier in his ranks. To win them to his cause, he needn't really know any of them. What he must do is put out the kind of energy they'll respect and obey. The same thing is true for us in our relation to the subconscious.

We needn't face each and every

mental foe of our conscious resolutions. What we need to do is address the subconscious with that kind of magnetic determination which will enlist its support.

In many cases, it is a mistake to get people to rummage about too much among their past traumas and suppressed inclinations. The general who pays too much heed to the dissidents in his army may find that, by excessive concern for their attitude, he only strengthens them in their negativity. He can't afford to ignore them, but he *can* so strengthen the morale of the troops generally that the negative voices no longer have an audience.

He can also, if in self-honesty

he finds their complaints justified, address the complaints without weakening his position by pampering the complainers.

Affirmation is a mighty weapon in the hands of anyone who uses it intelligently. Used unwisely, it can be a means of merely sweeping one's foibles under the carpet, as it were, instead of dealing with them. Used wisely, however, affirmation can be a means of confronting those foibles and commanding them to "shape up!"

What I did, without realizing it, in telling myself that I really *had* given up smoking at last, was address my subconscious.

For the subconscious is particularly open to conscious resolution at the moments of falling asleep and of awakening.

Perhaps you've noticed how, when you've fallen asleep with the thought, "I'm exhausted!" no matter how long you slept that night you were still tired when you awoke in the morning. If, on the other hand, no matter how tired you were, you fell asleep with the thought of how refreshed you'd be in the morning, the chances are that when you woke up the next day you really *did* feel refreshed.

When you want to affirm something, make a special point of doing so as you go to sleep. Carry that thought into the subconscious. The next morning as you wake up, while the subconscious is still open, make that affirmation again. You can change your life for the better, thereby, very quickly.

Meditation is one of the best ways of bringing the subconscious into alignment with one's conscious resolutions. The peace of meditation filters down into deeper-than-conscious layers of consciousness. The practice of meditation, moreover, brings on an awareness of the mind as a totality: subconscious, conscious, and also *superconscious* (that region where our highest inspirations dwell).

Our higher nature—the superconscious—is centered physically in the frontal lobe of the brain. The subconscious, similarly, is located at the back part of the brain and in the spine. Gradually, especially by meditation, one can learn to direct his resolution forward from this seat at the back of the brain to the point between the eyebrows. In this way, he can enlist his subconscious in the efforts of his will, rather than willing things only on a conscious level. It is important that he do so, for, indeed, the subconscious cannot be by-passed.

Thus, while meditating at the point between the eyebrows, it is helpful consciously to direct the flow of energy *from* the medulla oblongata—the seat also, incidentally, of the ego—toward the frontal lobe of the brain.

In taking the reader this far, however, I step beyond the bounds naturally assigned by the subject matter of this book. I encourage interested readers, therefore, to study others of my books, particularly my correspondence course, "The Art and Science of Raja Yoga."

For present purposes, a simple rule of affirmation will suffice. Repeat your affirmation over and over—loudly, at first, to command the attention of your thoughts; then more softly, to command their interest; then whisperingly, as if coaxing also the cooperation of your subconscious; then mentally only, drawing your subconscious thoughts and tendencies into your act of will. Then, finally, in deep inner silence, offer your resolution up to the superconscious, to your higher, soul-nature.

Two final suggestions will prove helpful: Make your affirmations rhythmic, in a rhythm commensurate with the nature of your resolution.

Secondly, make them positive. Don't say, for instance, "I *won't* smoke ever again." Say, "I've given up smoking." Say it with the thought that the problem no longer exists for you, that you are inwardly free from it.

A positive approach is important, both because negative affirmation affirms the reality you want to overcome, and because by positive affirmation you'll place yourself in tune with the commands of your higher nature.

For the nature of the superconscious is to be solution-oriented. To tune in to that aspect of your nature which, ultimately, can truly command your destiny—don't dwell on the problems you face. Don't, on the other hand, ignore your problems. But exert your will in the full expectation that a solution to every problem can be found.

You'll be amazed, if you follow this practice, how quickly the right answers come to you. You won't behold the fences around you any longer. They'll simply cease to exist for you. You'll see beyond them, to the broad meadows and high mountains of expanded awareness, and expanded power.

At all times, therefore, be solution-oriented!

Energy generates magnetism. The stronger the flow of energy, the greater the magnetism. It is magnetism, finally, that attracts to us all that we receive in life.

Our magnetism depends to a paramount extent on the positiveness with which we direct our will. Positive thoughts are magnetic; negative thoughts weaken our magnetism. A cheerful attitude is magnetic; discouragement is de-magnetizing. Hope is magnetic; despair is de-magnetizing. Love is magnetic; hatred and indifference dull our magnetism. Faith is magnetic; doubt destroys magnetism.

Be, therefore, always positive, always cheerful, always full of hope, faith, and love.

CHAPTER FOURTEEN

"Be Practical in Your Idealism"

I've put the title of this chapter in quotes because it was a piece of advice that Paramhansa Yogananda once gave me. Sound advice I found it to be, too.

For energy has to be directed toward practical fulfillment. "Desire, plus energy," is not enough. It must be, "Desire, plus energy, *directed toward fulfillment.*"

An ineffective direction of will power collapses inward upon itself, eventually. Ineffectiveness is discouraging to the will.

So often in life we set ourselves impossible goals. Far better would it be to attempt the possible, even if we consider it far short of our highest ideals. For little successes will strengthen us, and prepare us, finally, to win the truly great victories of life.

A few friends of mine, years ago, gave me an insight into how important it is to take one step at a time, and not to affirm a success that is too far beyond the limits of present realities. A safe rule, indeed, is not to exercise the power of faith more than one step beyond one's actual experience. These friends started a business that was to make them and everyone they knew wealthy. For a time it all sounded marvelous, if almost too good to be true. Firm believers in the power of positive thinking, they were affirming millions, when they were still in debt. Somehow, they told themselves, the immediate problems they faced would be crossed over by the over-arching bridge of exuberant faith.

Well, gradually I began to see that there were problems in their business which needed addressing with more than affirmations and positive thinking. Concerned, at last, for the very survival of their enterprise, I invited them all to my home for a consultation. There, I offered them a number of what I felt were practical suggestions that might still save the situation for them. They were all aware, by this time, that the business was on the verge of collapse.

All I got for my pains, unfortunately, was hostility. And so the business failed. It was almost as though they'd subconsciously *wanted* it to fail. Or perhaps all they wanted was the satisfaction of having tried to be successful, without the burden of actually running a successful enterprise. Perhaps, in other words, their attempt was only a sop to their conscience.

At any rate, my point in telling the story is what I learned from it. The first lesson was, as I said, the importance of combining affirmation and positive thinking with practicality. The second was the realization that inveterate dreamers tend to feel actually threatened by the need to be practical.

Perhaps they consider realism an offense to their ideals. As long, in other words, as their dream remains unsullied by facts, they feel they can keep it pure and lofty. They don't realize that the task of actualizing an idea doesn't necessarily besmirch it, or that realities are not necessarily compromising to idealism. Rather, it is only by coming to grips with reality and making it serve one's higher purpose that one can accomplish whatever good it is his lot in life to accomplish.

So then, do you want to attract money? Do you want to achieve success in your undertakings? Then be clear in your mind as to what it is you really want. Be clear in your mind, in your heart, in all your directions in life. In other words, work to develop crystal clarity.

The Bible tells us, "In all thy getting, get understanding." Whatever we do in life should be done *consciously,* not automatically, as a mere function of habit, or as a mere expression of other people's expectations of us.

In conclusion, I hope this little book will prove helpful to you in your efforts to develop that measure of understanding which alone will give you what you most truly want in life.

About the Author

J. Donald Walters founded and leads the world's largest network of intentional communities and has overseen the establishment of the well-known East West Bookshop chain, three publishing houses, several natural foods stores and restaurants, four schools, three world-renowned retreat centers, and a number of other small businesses, all of which continue to thrive and grow. His books and music recordings have sold over 3.5 million copies worldwide and are translated into 29 languages.

Index

FURTHER EXPLORATIONS

If you are inspired by *Money Magnetism* and would like to learn more about J. Donald Walters (Swami Kriyananda) and Paramhansa Yogananda and his teachings, Crystal Clarity Publishers offers many additional resources to assist you.

Business and Career

MATERIAL SUCCESS THROUGH YOGA PRINCIPLES

A Twenty-Six Lesson Study-at-Home Program

Swami Kriyananda (J. Donald Walters)

This course condenses the experience of nearly sixty years of work—organizing, building, and creating out of "thin air" seven of the largest and most successful intentional communities in the world today.

These lessons compellingly communicate that spirituality and material success are not separate, unrelated aspects of life, but that they, in truth, help each other. By following yoga principles, you can have all the benefits of true success: happiness, inner peace, understanding, true friendships, and life's normal comforts without the suffocation of meaningless luxury.

Each of the twenty-six lessons is packed with information, examples, stories, inspiration, and solutions to common problems that face every person seeking success.

By applying the principles and practices taught in this course, business, government, and educational leaders will be better prepared to guide our future directions with dignity, right action, and success. It is also of immense help to the millions who suffer from work-related stress, and who seek a more balanced approach to personal satisfaction through their work.

Praise for the MATERIAL SUCCESS COURSE

"[This] is a significant contribution to the transformation of human awareness. . . . [and] provides the platform on which ethics and practicality meet, each strengthening the other. I sincerely recommend that business and government leaders who want to be morally, psychologically, and practically prepared for the challenges that face our world study this course and apply its lessons with all due urgency, making it part of their training program for leaders of tomorrow."

—Professor Ervin Laszlo, Nobel Peace Prize Nominee,
Founder and President, Club of Budapest

"I knew I had tapped into teachings that were very relevant and immediately applicable to my work as a manager in a large government agency. I read each lesson at home, and then brought the handy booklet with me to work and kept it on my desk for reference and to remind me of the key points in that lesson. I could reflect on these while at work and feel immediately inspired and recharged."

—Russ Reece, Director, Corporate Planning Bureau,
California Franchise Tax Board

"My goal as an International Business Consultant is to make my clients successful through the application of modern American business practices and technology know-how. Working in harmony with these spiritual principles is already bearing fruit in the success attained by my clients and myself."

—Simon Hartley, Consulting Practice Manager, Red Hat Corporation

"As a project manager for a big engineering project, I am applying the principles of 'non-attachment' and 'people are more important than things' and finding that they are giving me amazing results. The feeling of joy that I experience throughout my day, whether it be during meetings or even in heated discussions, is directly due to the training I have received in this course."

—Arnab Chatterjee, Project Manager, IT Department, Boeing Corporation

If you would like more information on this course, please contact Crystal Clarity Publishers: 800.424.1055 or 530.478.7600, or www.ananda.org/successthroughyoga

The Art of Supportive Leadership

A Practical Guide for People in Positions of Responsibility

J. Donald Walters

You can learn to be a more effective leader by viewing leadership in terms of shared accomplishments rather than personal advancement. Drawn from timeless Eastern wisdom, this book is clear, concise, and practical—designed from the start to produce results quickly and simply.

Used in training seminars in the U.S., Europe, and India, this book gives practical advice for leaders and potential leaders to help increase effectiveness, creativity, and team building. Individual entrepreneurs, corporations such as Kellogg, military and police personnel, and non-profit organizations are using this approach.

Praise for The Art of Supportive Leadership

"We've been looking for something like this for a long time. We use it in our Managers' Training Workshop. This book is very practical, very readable, and concise. Highly recommended!"

—Kellogg Corporation

"*The Art of Supportive Leadership* stands out among business books. I recommend it. It makes for good reading with a good message."

—*Executive Book Summaries*

"This book is a gem! What he says can be put into practice immediately."

—*Human Resources Development Review*

"The most depth and understanding of what a manager faces of the many management books I've read over the years. I plan to keep it on my desk as a daily reference."

—*Ray Narragon, Sun Microsystems*

"Profound principles in leadership. Penetrating insights for current and aspiring managers alike."

—*Mike Sage, Stanford University Medical School*

Intuition for Starters

How to Know and Trust Your Inner Guidance

J. Donald Walters

Every day we are confronted with difficult problems or complicated situations for which there are no easy intellectual answers. At these moments, we all wish for another way to know how to make the right choice.

There is another way: through using our intuition. More than just a "feeling" or a guess, true intuition is one of the most important—yet often least developed—of our human faculties.

Intuition for Starters straightforwardly explains what true intuition is and where it comes from, describes the attitudes necessary for developing it, and gives you easy-to-understand practices and guidelines that will help you tap into intuitive guidance at will.

Praise for INTUITION FOR STARTERS

"*Intuition for Starters* is a small book on the basics of intuition and following your intuition. . . . This is the only book I have seen on intuition that effectively explains how to know when something is intuition and when it is not. Learning to discern when something is truly your intuition speaking to you and when it is not is critically important if you are to trust you intuition. This is a recommended read because the discussion of discerning intuition is so well done."

—*Midwest Book Review*

"I'm indebted to this book for clarifying what intuition actually is and for giving solid guidance in becoming more intuitive. Walters offers exercises for tapping into the superconscious (the source of intuition), for obtaining greater awareness of chakras, and more. Based in part on the teaching of Paramhansa Yogananda, this book is an excellent beginning point for anyone who wants to understand or better utilize innate, yet undeveloped, intuitive skills."

—*NAPRA Review*

The Yogananda Wisdom series

HOW TO BE A SUCCESS

The Wisdom of Yogananda, Volume 4

Paramhansa Yogananda

Is there a power that can reveal hidden veins of riches and uncover treasures of which we have never dreamed? Is there a force that we can call upon to give health, happiness, and spiritual enlightenment?

In this book of Yogananda's original writings, not available elsewhere, Paramhansa Yogananda shares how we can tap into our own inner powers for achieving the highest material and spiritual success.

This is the fourth volume in **The Wisdom of Yogananda series**, the series devoted to sharing the Master's expansive and compassionate wisdom, his sense of fun, and his practical spiritual guidance. Titles include: ***How to Be Happy All the Time, Karma and Reincarnation, and Spiritual Relationships.***

Paramhansa Yogananda is best known as the author *Autobiography of a Yogi*, which has sold millions of copies worldwide, and is widely recognized as a spiritual classic. One of the first to bring yoga teachings to the West, he is considered one of the most influential spiritual teachers of the 20th century.

Paramhansa Yogananda

AUTOBIOGRAPHY OF A YOGI

Original 1946 Edition

Paramhansa Yogananda

Yogananda's *Autobiography* has entered the homes and hearts of millions of people all over the world. This Crystal Clarity publication is a verbatim reprinting of the original 1946 edition. Subsequent editions include revisions made after the author's death. Now it is possible to read the first edition, with all its inherent power, just as the great Master originally intended it.

Praise for AUTOBIOGRAPHY OF A YOGI

"In the original edition, published during Yogananda's life, one is more in contact with Yogananda himself. While Yogananda founded centers and organizations, his concern was more with guiding individuals to direct communion with Divinity rather than with promoting any one church as opposed to another. This spirit is easier to grasp in the original edition of this great spiritual and yogic classic."

—David Frawley, Director, American Institute of Vedic Studies

Autobiography of a Yogi is one of the best-selling spiritual biographies of all time. Now, for the first time, Paramhansa Yogananda's thrilling autobiography is accessible for your inspiration in this beautiful full-color card deck and booklet.

Autobiography of a Yogi Card Deck

52 cards and booklet

Paramhansa Yogananda

Each of the 52 cards features an inspiring quotation taken from the text of the Original 1946 First Edition—the preferred edition for both enthusiasts and collectors. The flip side of each card features a photograph from the book or a previously unreleased and rare photograph of Yogananda. For the first time, these famous images and quotations will be portable, and can be used in your home, journal, auto, and purse. The enclosed booklet includes a history of the Autobiography, additional information about the quotations and photographs, and a user's guide for the card deck.

Autobiography of a Yogi

by Paramhansa Yogananda, read by Swami Kriyananda

Audiobook, Unabridged

This is a recording of the original, unedited 1946 edition of *Autobiography of a Yogi*, presented on 16 CDs. Read by Swami Kriyananda, this is the only audio edition that is read by one of Yogananda's direct disciples—someone who both knew him and was directly trained by him.

Swami Kriyananda (J. Donald Wlaters)

One of the best known of Yogananda's disciples is J. Donald Walters (Swami Kriyananda), the founder of Ananda and Crystal Clarity Publishers. Walter's autobiography, a sequel of sorts to *Autobiography of a Yogi*, contains hundreds of stories about Yogananda, culled from the nearly four years that Kriyananda lived with and was trained by Yogananda. It offers the unique perspective of a disciple reflecting on his time with a great Master.

The Path—My Life with Paramhansa Yogananda

One Man's Search on the Only Path There Is

Swami Kriyananda (J. Donald Walters)

The Path is the moving story of Kriyananda's years with Paramhansa Yogananda. *The Path* completes Yogananda's life story and includes more than 400 never-before-published stories about Yogananda, India's emissary to the West and the first yoga master to spend the greater part of his life in America.

Praise for THE PATH

"Perfectly captures the personality of Paramhansa Yogananda. I am delighted that my brother disciple has produced this monumental work. I highly recommend *The Path*."

—Roy Eugene Davis, Founder, Center for Spiritual Awareness

If you would like to learn how to begin your own practice of meditation, as taught by Yogananda and Kriyananda, we recommend the following title.

MEDITATION FOR STARTERS

Swami Kriyananda (J. Donald Walters)

Meditation brings balance into our lives, providing an oasis of profound rest and renewal. Doctors are prescribing it for a variety of stress-related diseases. This award-winning book offers simple but powerful guidelines for attaining inner peace. Learn to prepare the body and mind for meditation with special breathing techniques and ways to focus the mind, develop superconscious awareness, strengthen your willpower, improve your intuition, and increase your calmness.

Praise for MEDITATION FOR STARTERS

"*Meditation for Starters* is one of the best introductions to meditation for the beginner."

—YOGA INTERNATIONAL

"A gentle guide to entering the most majestic, fulfilling dimensions of consciousness. Walters is a wise teacher whose words convey love and compassion. Read and listen and allow your life to change."

—Larry Dossey, M.D., author of PRAYER IS GOOD MEDICINE

"*Meditation for Starters* is J. Donald Walters at his best!"

—*Louise Hay, author of* YOU CAN HEAL YOUR LIFE

"Hang on to the silken cord of Walters' smooth words and/or voice and learn how to increase concentration, willpower, intuition, and superconscious awareness."

–TOTAL HEALTH *magazine*

Crystal Clarity also makes available many music and audiobook resources. Here are some that you might find helpful to increase your energy or to create an atmosphere of peace and inspiration for your office.

POWER CHANTS

Ananda Kirtan

Unlock your divine strength and energy. Chanting is an ancient technique for uplifting the mind into higher states of consciousness. This recording will help you tap into the positive aspects of power—the ability to strengthen and direct your will and creative energy, and to channel your energy toward God.

"You feel as if you have been dropped in the center of a lively kirtan gathering, where all those around you are immersed in the sacred energy of the moment. Perfect for reaching higher states of consciousness, prayer, and lifting the spirits.

—Music Design

Relax: Meditations for Flute and Cello

With David Eby and Sharon Brooks

Donald Walters, composer

Experience tranquility and inner peace. Much more than just beautiful background music, *Relax: Meditations for Flute and Cello* takes you on a journey deep within, helping you to experience a dynamic sense of peace and calmness. *Relax* is specifically designed to slow respiration and heart rate, and bring you to your calm center. The recording features fifteen melodies on flute and cello, accompanied by harp, guitar, keyboard, and strings.

David Eby, cellist for the internationally renowned group Pink Martini, joins the highly acclaimed flutist Sharon Brooks for their second recording. In addition to giving concerts together throughout the U.S. and abroad, they are both highly sought-after recording artists.

AUM: Mantra of Eternity

Chanted by Swami Kriyananda

This recording features nearly 70 minutes of continuous vocal chanting of AUM, the Sanskrit word for the cosmic creative vibration. AUM is discussed extensively by Yogananda in *Autobiography of a Yogi and is* chanted here by his disciple Kriyananda. This recording is a stirring way to tune into the cosmic power of AUM.

Crystal Clarity Publishers

Timeless Truths

When you're seeking a book on practical spiritual living, you want to know it's based on an authentic tradition of timeless teachings and resonates with integrity.

This is the goal of Crystal Clarity Publishers: to offer you books of practical wisdom filled with true spiritual principles that have not only been tested through the ages but also through personal experience.

Started in 1968, Crystal Clarity is the publishing house of Ananda, a spiritual community dedicated to meditation and living by true values, as shared by Paramhansa Yogananda, and his direct disciple Swami Kriyananda, the founder of Ananda. The members of our staff and each of our authors live by these principles. Our worldwide work touches thousands whose lives have been enriched by these universal teachings.

We publish only books that combine creative thinking, universal principles, and a timeless message. Crystal Clarity books will open doors to help you discover more fulfillment and joy by living and acting from the center of peace within you.

To request a catalog, place an order for the products you read about in the Further Explorations section of this book, or to find out more information about us and our products, please contact us:

Crystal Clarity Publishers
14618 Tyler Foote Road
Nevada City, CA 95959
T: 800.424.1055 / 530.478.7600
F: 530.478.7610
clarity@crystalclarity.com
www.crystalclarity.com

For our online catalog, complete with secure ordering, please visit us on the web at: www.crystalclarity.com. Crystal Clarity Publishers' music and audiobooks are available on all the popular online download services. Look for us in your favorite online music catalog.

Ananda is one of the most successful networks of intentional communities in the world. Urban communities have been developed in Sacramento and Palo Alto (CA), Seattle (WA), Portland (OR), as well as a retreat center and European community in Assisi, Italy and a center and community near New Delhi, India. The Expanding Light, a guest retreat for spiritual studies visited by over 2,000 people each year, offers courses in Self-realization and related subjects.

Ananda Sangha Contact Information

mail: 14618 Tyler Foote Road
Nevada City, CA 95959

phone: 530.478.7560
online: www.ananda.org
email: sanghainfo@ananda.org

Ananda's guest retreat, The Expanding Light, offers a varied, year round schedule of classes and workshops on yoga, meditation, and spiritual practice. You may also come for a relaxed personal renewal, participating in ongoing activities as much or as little as you wish.

The beautiful serene mountain setting, supportive staff, and delicious vegetarian food provide an ideal environment for a truly meaningful, spiritual vacation.

Expanding Light Contact Information

phone: 800.346.5350
online: www.expandinglight.org
email: info@expandinglight.org

Made in the USA